CANADIAN CONTEMPORARY REPERTOIRE SERIES

FUN SELECTIONS OF JAZZ - POP - LATIN - FOLK

LEVEL FOUR

CONSERVATORY CANADA™

For more information about Conservatory Canada
and its programs visit our website at:
www.conservatorycanada.ca

Office of the Registrar
Conservatory Canada
45 King Street, Suite 61
London, Ontario, Canada
N6A 1B8

FONDATION
SOCAN
FOUNDATION

© 2010 Conservatory Canada
Published and Distributed by Novus Via Music Group Inc.
All Rights Reserved.

ISBN 978-1-49500-539-8

Novus Via Music Group Inc.
189 Douglas Street, Stratford, Ontario, Canada N5A 5P8
(519) 273-7520 www.NVmusicgroup.com

Preface

Canadian Contemporary Repertoire Series: Fun Selections of Jazz, Pop, Latin and Folk Music Level Four is an exciting series of piano works by Canadian Composers. Level Four offers grade four and five students twenty-nine appealing pieces at varied levels within the grade requirements. Students will develop technical and musical skills with user friendly repertoire from an entrance level to grade five works.

Repertoire selections have been based on grade appropriate keys, time signatures, accompaniment figures, degree of difficulty and length. Jazz styles include preparatory rags like *The Out-of-Breath Rag*, which leads comfortably to *Rocky Mountain Rag* complete with stride bass, syncopated melodies and octave displacement. Boogies include works like *Blindside Boogie*. *Alberta Blues* and *Pentatonic Blues* provide varied accompaniments and blues scale playing. Students will be delighted by the swing rhythm of works like *Jitterbug*, *Just Jumpin'* and *Swingin' Ain't Easy*. The lovely jazz ballad *The River Meets the Sea*, jazz prelude *Emotional Performance* and jazz waltz *Joy* are just some of the jazz titles offered in this collection.

The ever popular work *The Entertainer* has also been included in this collection. Students will be rockin' to titles like *Bring the Funk* and *Late Night Reggae*, while Latin dance rhythms are included in works like *Baila Conmigo por Favor* and *España*. Arrangements of folk songs *Taking Back Gear in the Night* and *Blooming Bright Star of Belle Isle* provide a strong sense of Canada's musical Heritage.

Conservatory Canada wants to keep music students studying longer! We understand the benefits gained through the study of music and we believe that students will remain engaged and excited about their studies if that music is current and familiar.

This is why we developed the Contemporary Idioms curriculum. Students can now be assessed and accredited through a program that involves contemporary styles of music such as Swing, Blues, Latin and Rock.

Conservatory Canada supports Canadian composers. This book contains pieces that are either original compositions or arrangements by Canadian musicians. All the selections in this book are eligible for a Conservatory Canada Contemporary Idioms examination. The pieces have been chosen with attention to proper pedagogy, skill development and student appeal. We hope you enjoy them!

TABLE OF CONTENTS

1 Mississippi, 2 Mississippi

Martha Hill Duncan

Searching

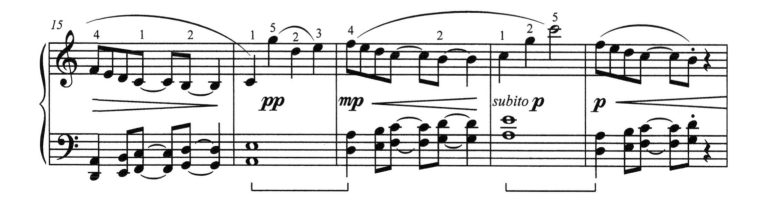

1 Mississippi, 2 Mississippi   2 / 2

Alberta Blues

Joyce Pinckney

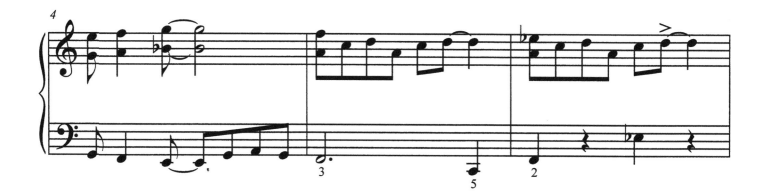

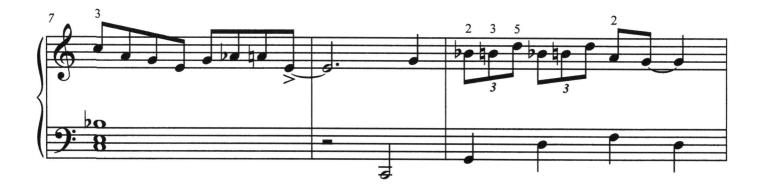

Alberta Blues 2 / 2

Baila Conmigo por Favor

Please Dance With Me

Andrew Harbridge

Allegro Moderato

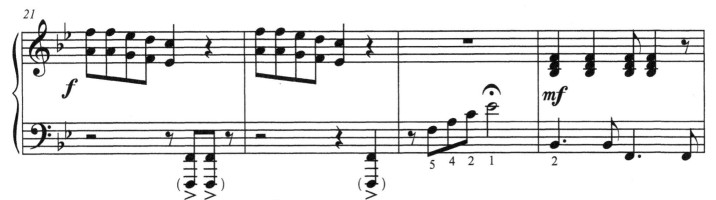

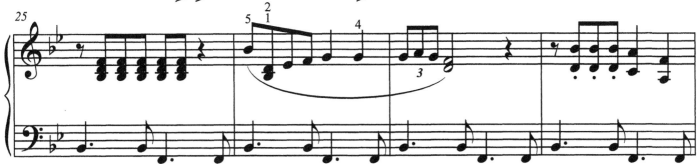

Baila Conmogo por Favor 2 / 2

Blindside Boogie

Tyler Seidenberg

Quick Swing

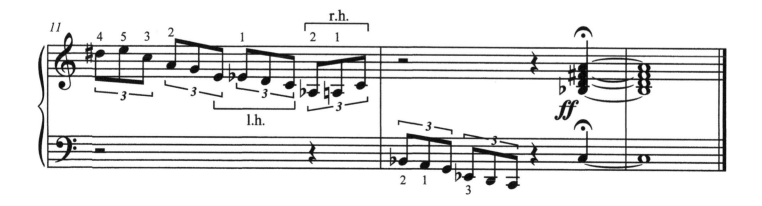

Bring the Funk

Tyler Seidenberg

Chanson de la Nuit

Sheila Tyrrell

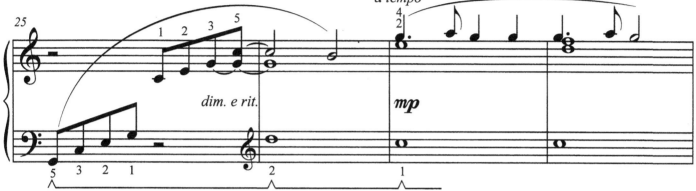

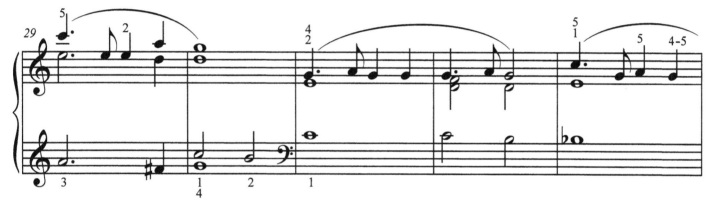

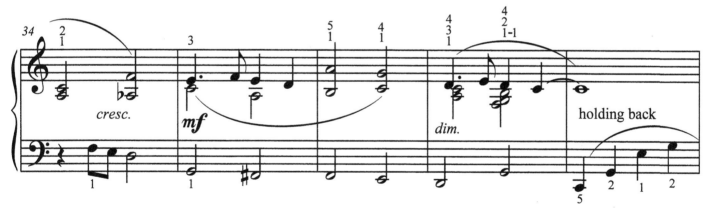

Dance of the Raindrops

An E minor Pentatonic Scale Study

Andrew Harbridge

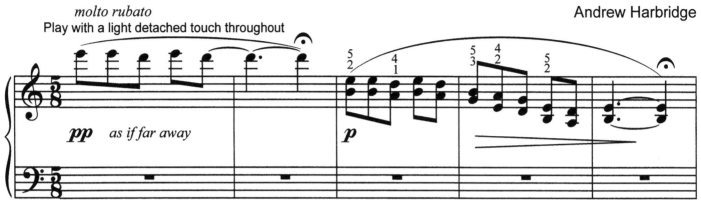

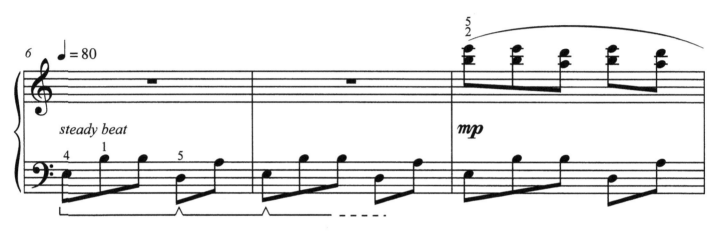

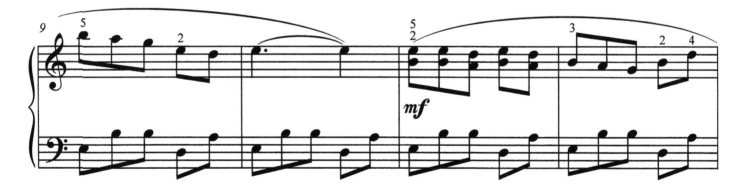

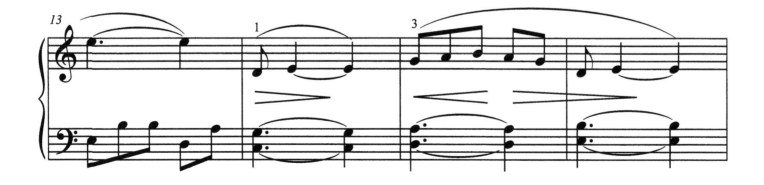

morendo

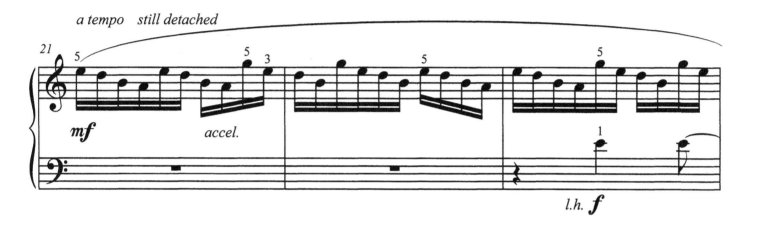

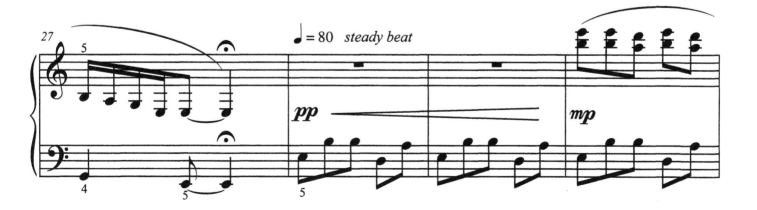

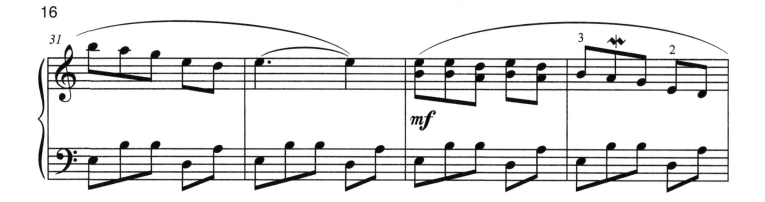

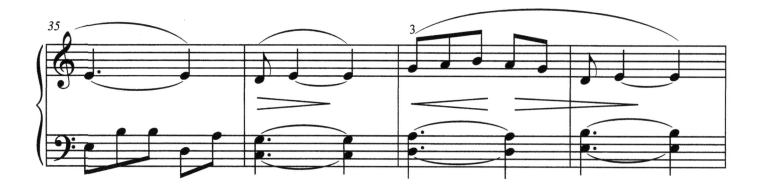

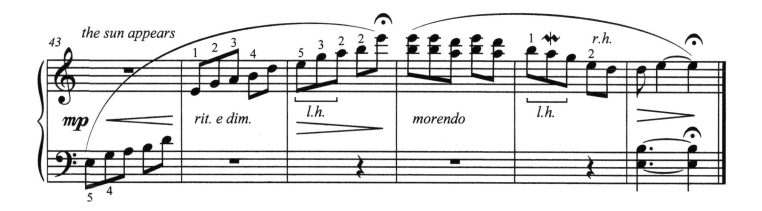

Jazzy Black Fleece

arr. Joyce Pinckney

Giving Generously

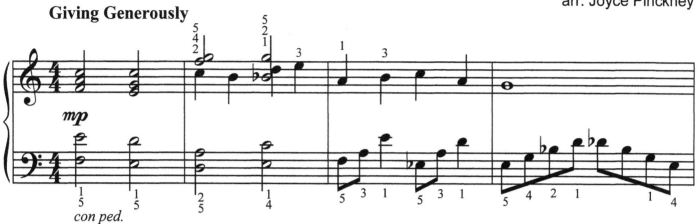

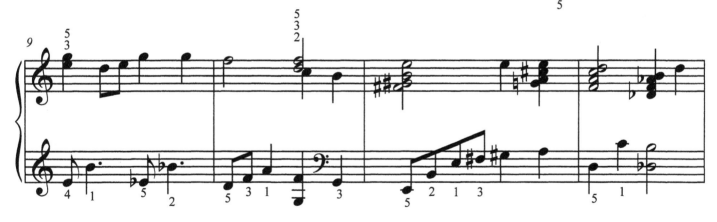

Emotional Performance

Fishel Pustilnik

Tenderly

con ped.

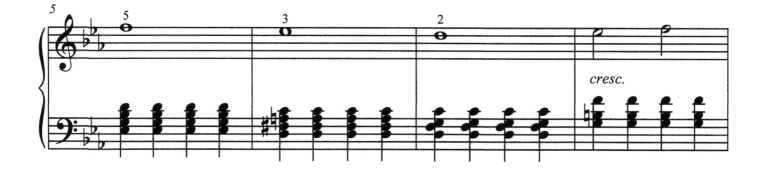

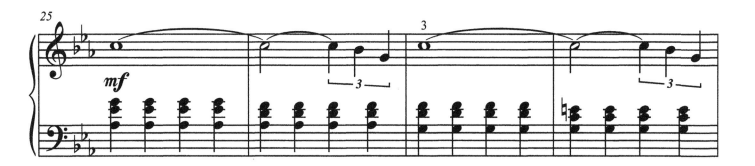

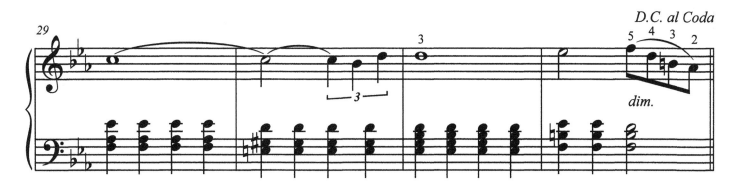

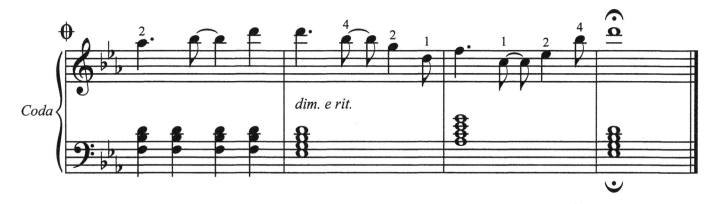

España

Debra Wanless

Hotly

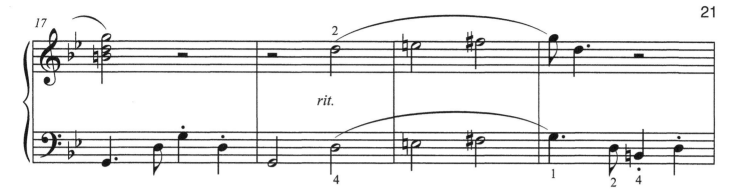

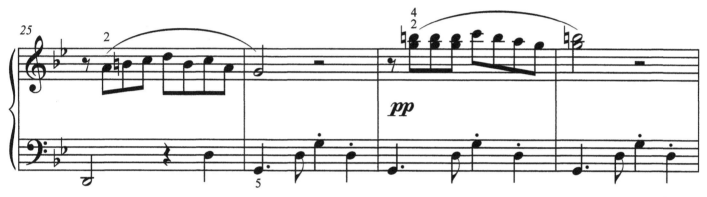

España 2 / 2

Gadabout

Sheila Tyrrell

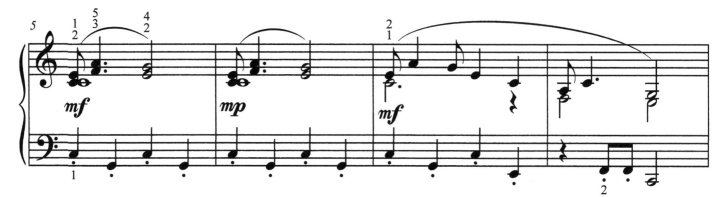

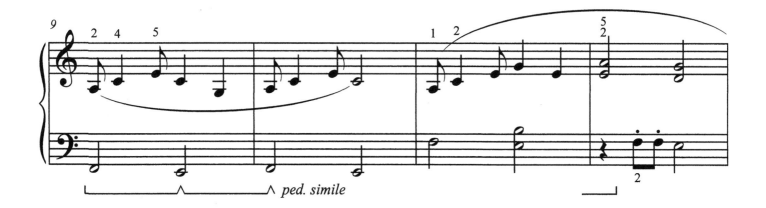

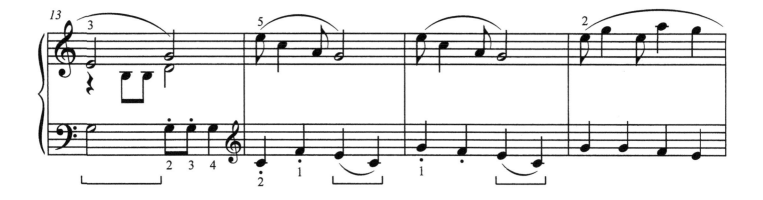

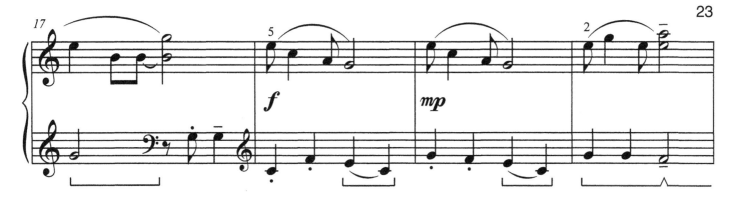

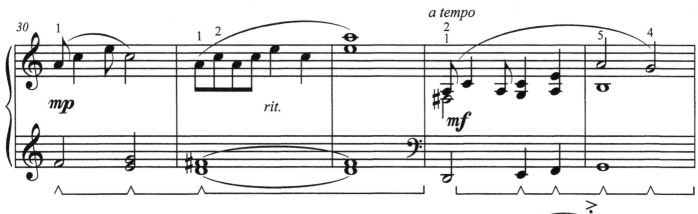

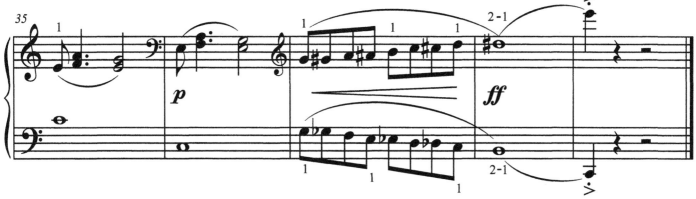

Gadabout 2 / 2

Hazy Afternoon

Joseph Chung

Reflective

ped. simile

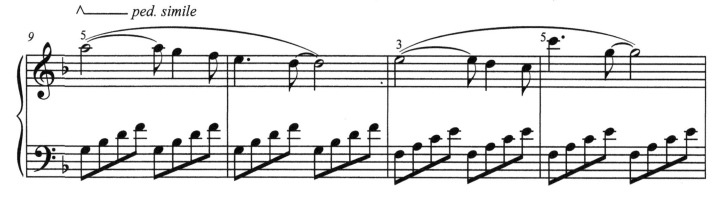

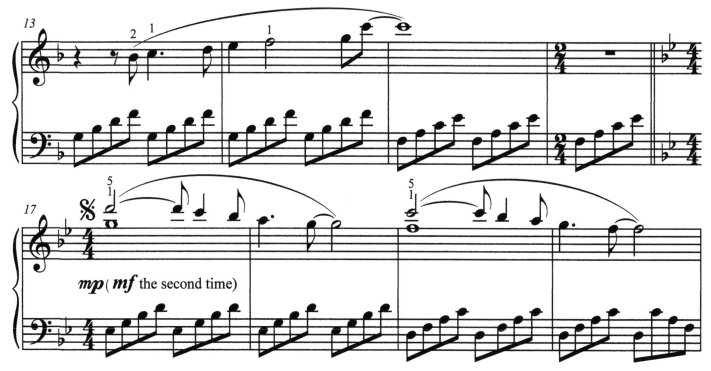

ped. come prima

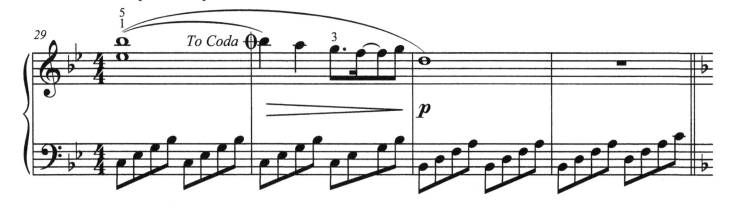

To Coda

G m7   Fmaj7   *D.S. al Coda*

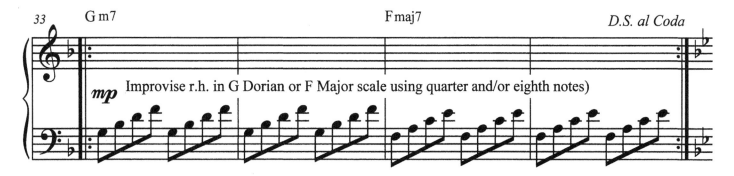

mp Improvise r.h. in G Dorian or F Major scale using quarter and/or eighth notes)

Coda   rit.   *p*   *pp*

Jitterbug

Beverly Porter

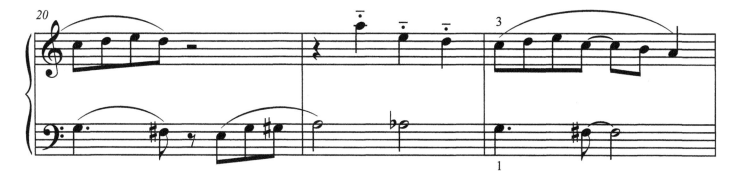

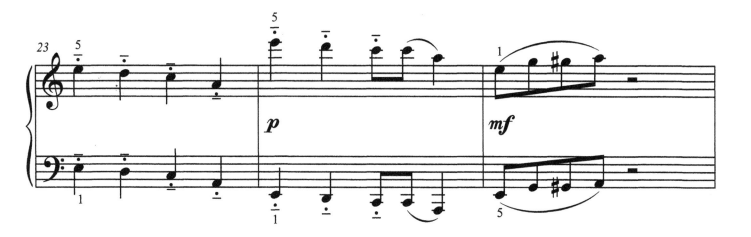

Slower

Joy

Geoff Peters

Medium Jazz Waltz, Swing Feel

Taking Back Gear in the Night

Canadian Folk Song

Just Jumpin'

Brian Usher

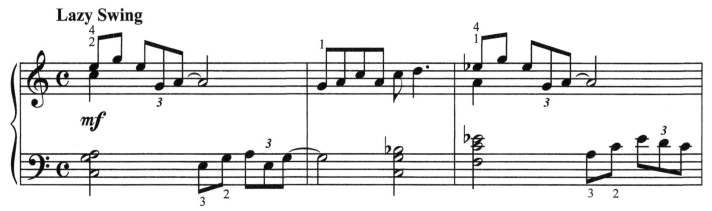

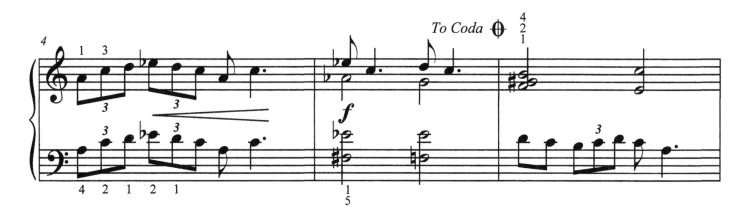

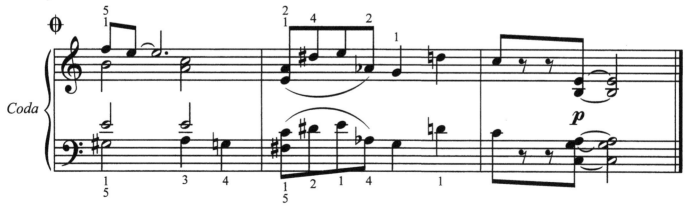

Mary Had a Cool Jazz Lamb

Joyce Pinckney

Pedal harmonically with a light foot

Swing

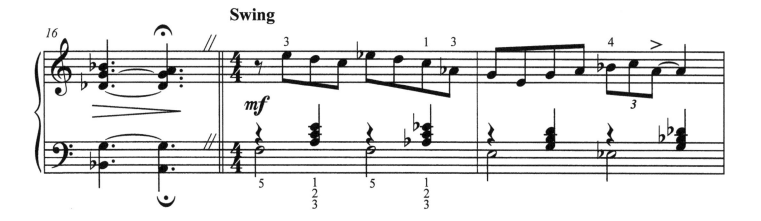

Mary Had a Cool Jazz Lamb 2 / 2

Melancholy Song

Andrew Harbridge

Pensive with some use of rubato

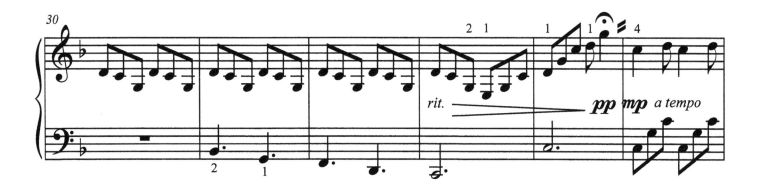

Melancholy Song 2 / 2

Moonlight Promenade

Debra Wanless

Strolling Along, swing the eighths

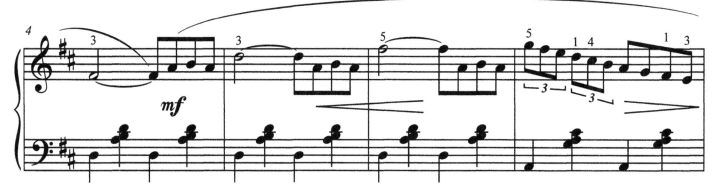

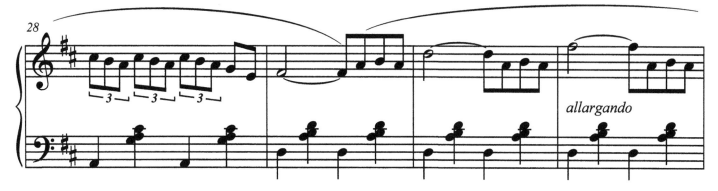

Moonlight Promenade 2 / 2

Party Jam

Debra Wanless

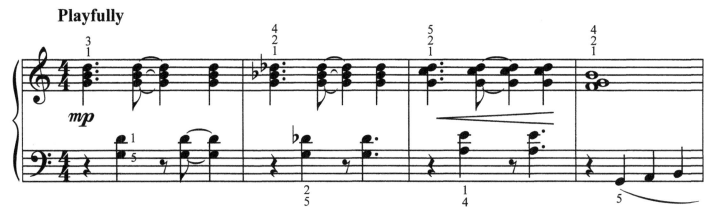

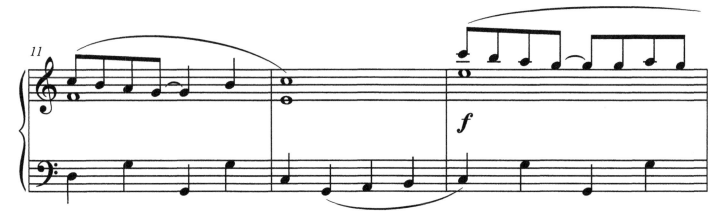

Party Jam 2 / 3

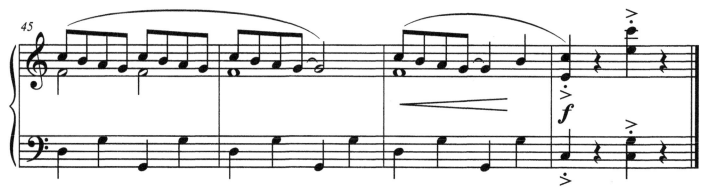

The Blooming Bright Star of Belle Isle

Canadian Folk Song

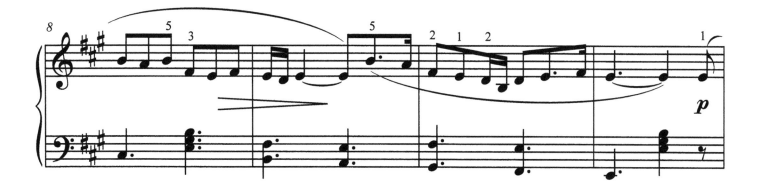

Pentatonic Blues

Andrew Harbridge

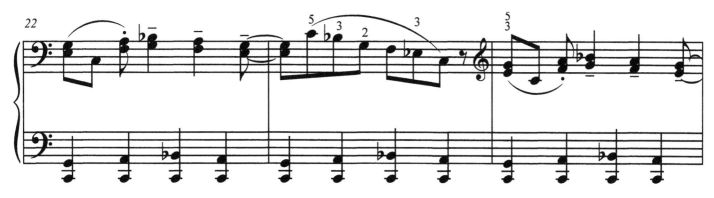

Pentatonic Blues 2 / 2

Rocky Mountain Rag

Joyce Pinckney

Play eighths evenly

l.h. *legato*

Rocky Mountain Rag 2 / 2

Swingin' Ain't Easy

Tyler Seidenberg

Swing It!

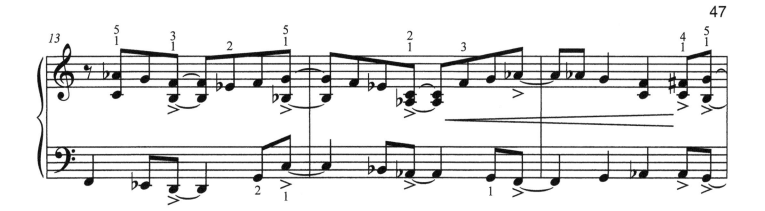

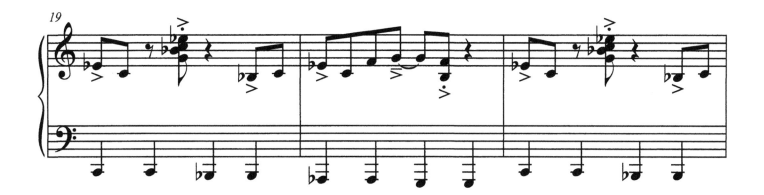

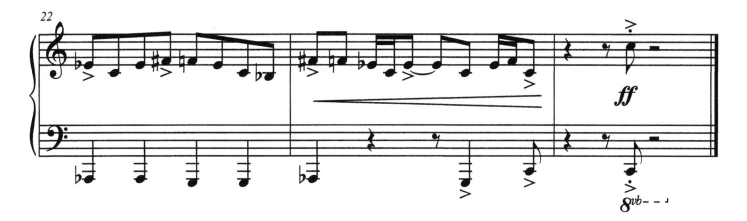

The Cracked Sound Board Blues

Rémi Bouchard

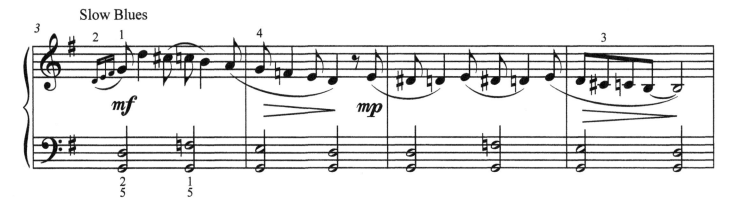

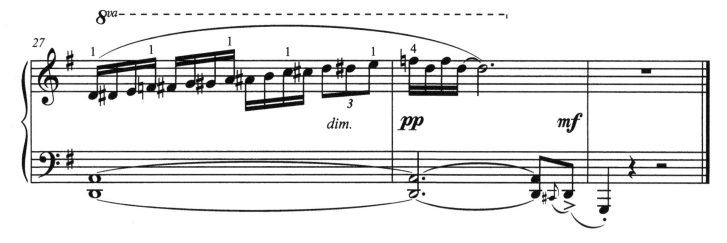

The Cracked Sound Board Blues 2 / 2

The Out-of-Breath Rag

Brian Usher

Bright Rag Tempo

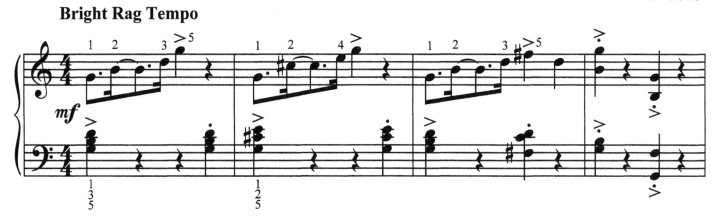

The Out-of-Breath Rag 2 / 2

Late Night Reggae

Tyler Seidenberg

Late Night Reggae 2 / 2

The Entertainer

A Ragtime in Two Step

Scott Joplin
(1868 - 1917)
arr. Debra Wanless

Moderato

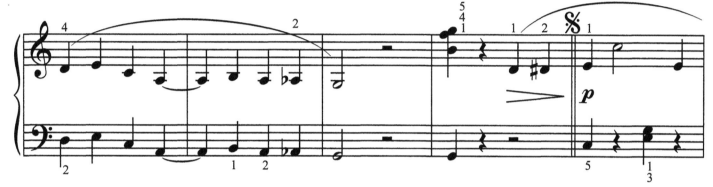

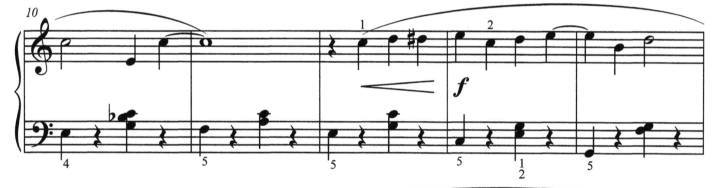

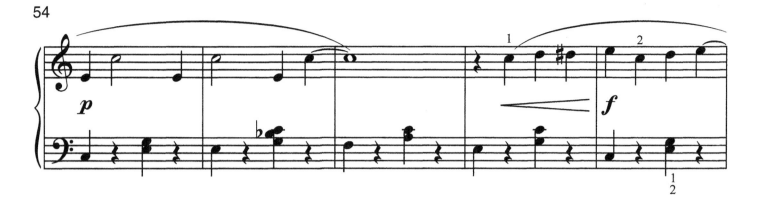

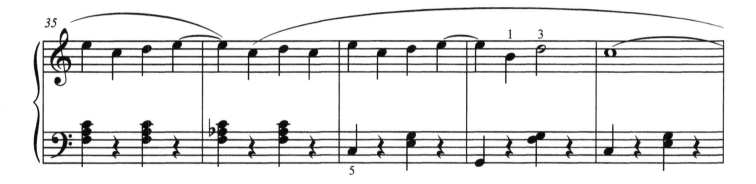

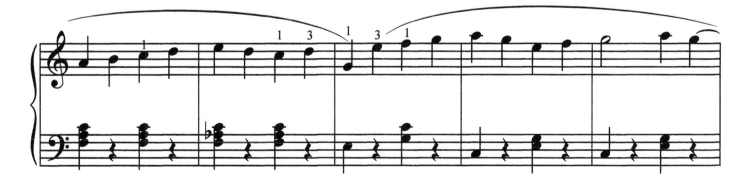

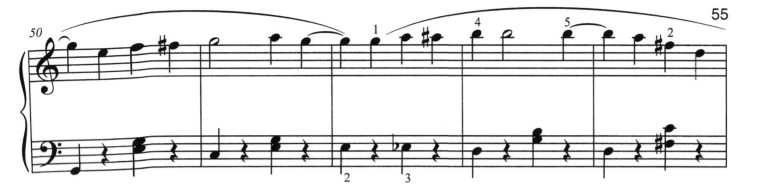

D.S. al Fine

The Entertainer 3 / 3

The River Meets the Sea

Andrew Harbridge

Gently and flowing

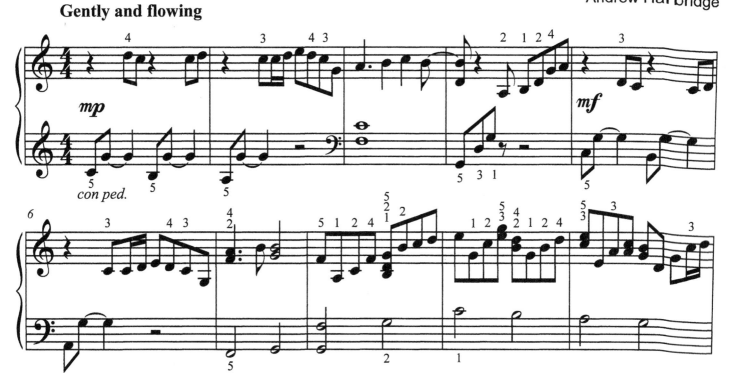